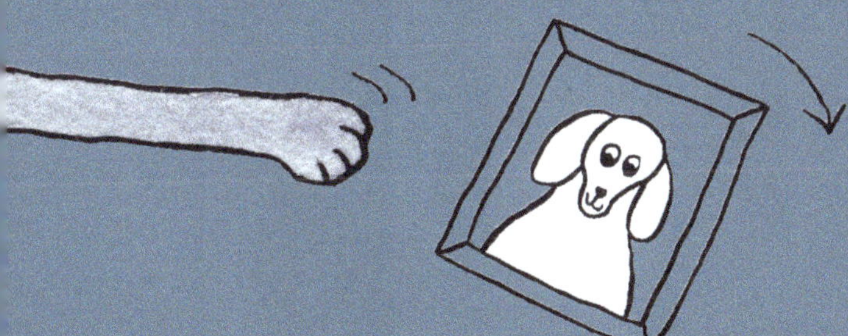

HOW TO LOVE A HUMAN

25 TIPS From A RUSSIAN BLUE To Other Cool Cats

By PAULA ROSECKY
Illustrations by MONICA HANLIN

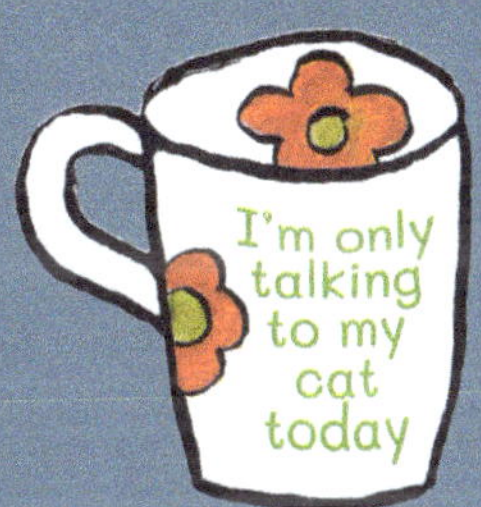

DEDICATED TO
LUDVIK, ZEN-JI AND ZÜMER

PAULA ROSECKY
Hello@PaulaRosecky.com

Illustrations and design by MONICA HANLIN. **Monica@CreamsicleStudios.com**

Ordering Information:
Special discounts are available on quantity purchases by corporations, associations, and others. For details, contact the "Special Sales Department" at the address above.

How To Love A Human/ Paula Rosecky. — 1st ed.
Paperback ISBN 979-8-9852630-0-8
eBook ISBN 979-8-9852630-1-5

It goes without saying that this book wouldn't be in existence without the companionship and love of my Russian Blues. Over the years, I've had three stunning Russian Blues named LUKVIK, ZEN-JI (Master of Zen) and ZÜMER. Each one of them had their own unique personalities. Each of them warmed my heart, made me smile and kept me centered. Their almost doglike loyalty, playfulness and, of course, stunning looks, made each one of them a truly unique creature and superb companion.

In early September 2020, I endeavored to write a book to support my business. Inspired by some precious letters my family wrote to my parents when they immigrated to the U.S., I had a loose plan to write a book that tied that experience to my coaching practice.

But, on a dark, early morning when I woke to write, I was enthusiastically greeted by my Russian Blue, ZÜMER. As he demanded my attention, I was struck with this much sillier *How to Love a Human* idea. In about 30 minutes I had the whole tiny book outlined and concepted. I laughed so hard my husband thought something was wrong with me. It was the kind of laugh that seems possessed. I laughed so hard I cried. I love it when that happens (it reminds me of my dad's laugh, may he rest in peace) and I was craving more laughter at the time.

the idea was just silly enough to take seriously

After releasing my self-judgment for shifting from "I should write a business book" to a "This is just so fun" book, I decided to go with it! It felt like divine intervention.

I had a vision of my friend, MONICA HANLIN, illustrating it. Over the course of two months, we had so much fun creating it. I wrote the copy and Monica illustrated the scenes, then whipped out the adorable layout. It was a joy to see her vision of how my copy came to life. I am so grateful for her talent, creativity, and lightheartedness.

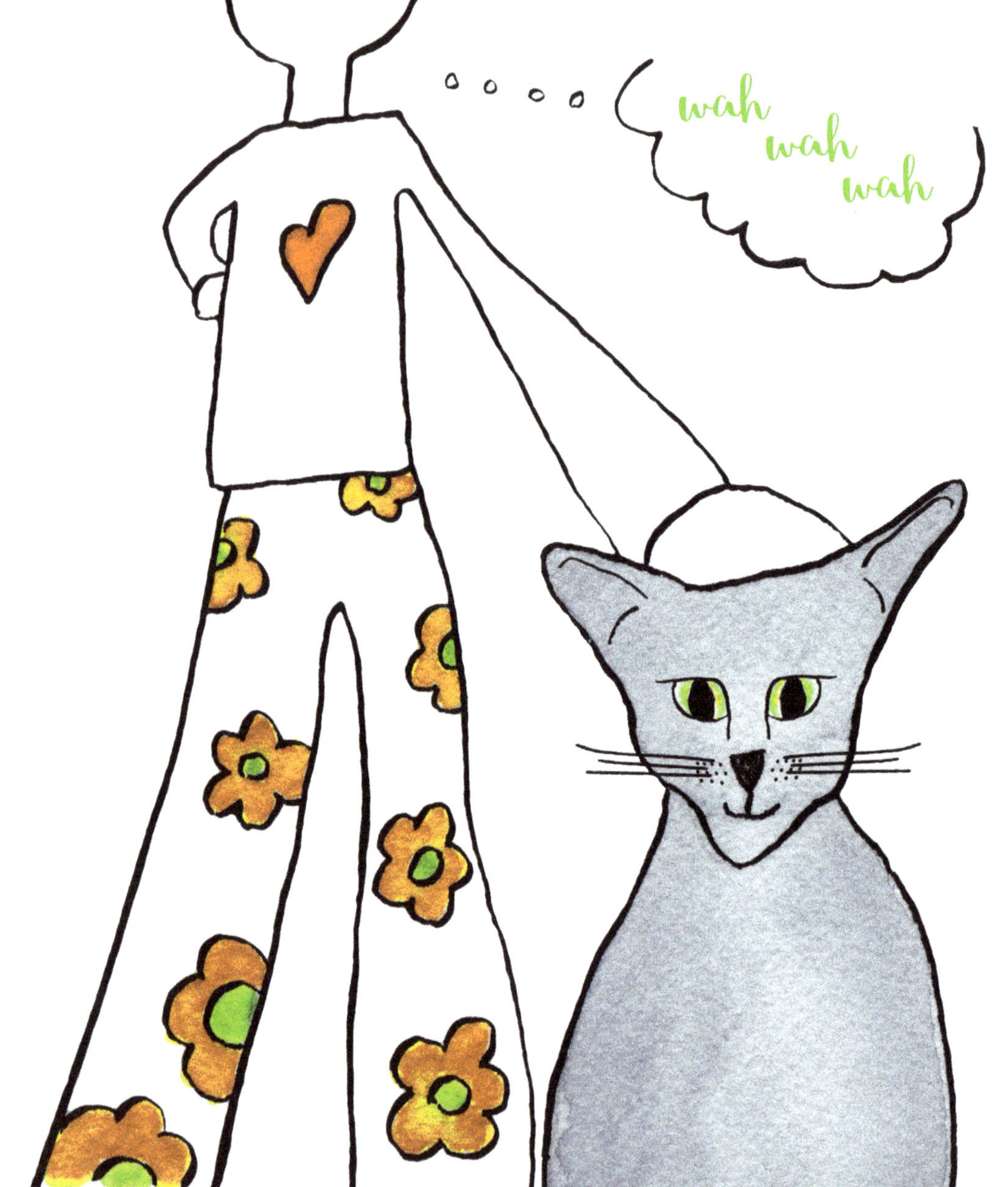
wah
wah
wah

Humans are the creatures with heads, hearts and limbs that tower over us. They **FEED US, SCOOP OUR POOP,** and **KEEP US SAFE.** They seem to think they're communicating with us when they make sounds you'll hear as "**WAH WAH WAH**".

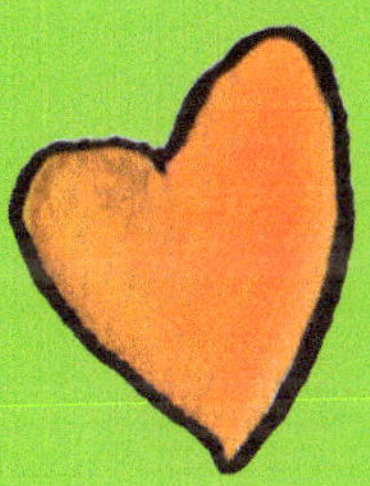

LOVE ALL THE HUMANS.

When they first bring you into their home, do NOT hide in the nooks and crannies of the underground space they will call the **BASEMENT.**

THEY WILL THINK YOU RAN AWAY AND WILL CALL ALL THE NEIGHBORS TO LOOK FOR YOU.

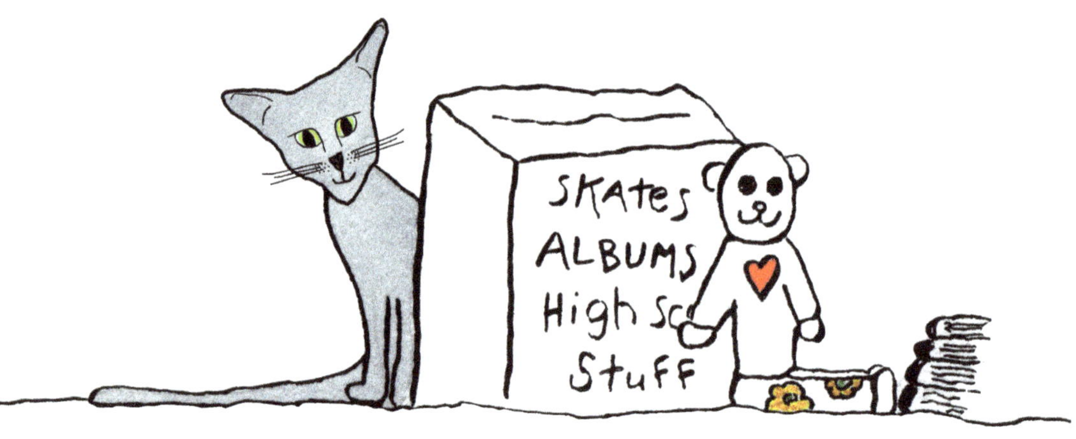

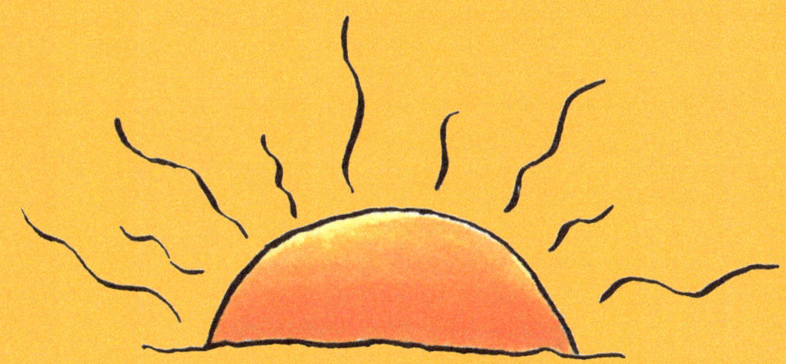

Let the humans know what time the sun comes up by caterwauling. They might be wearing plugs in their ears, so keep going until they **GET OUT OF BED.**

JUMPING ON THEM HELPS.

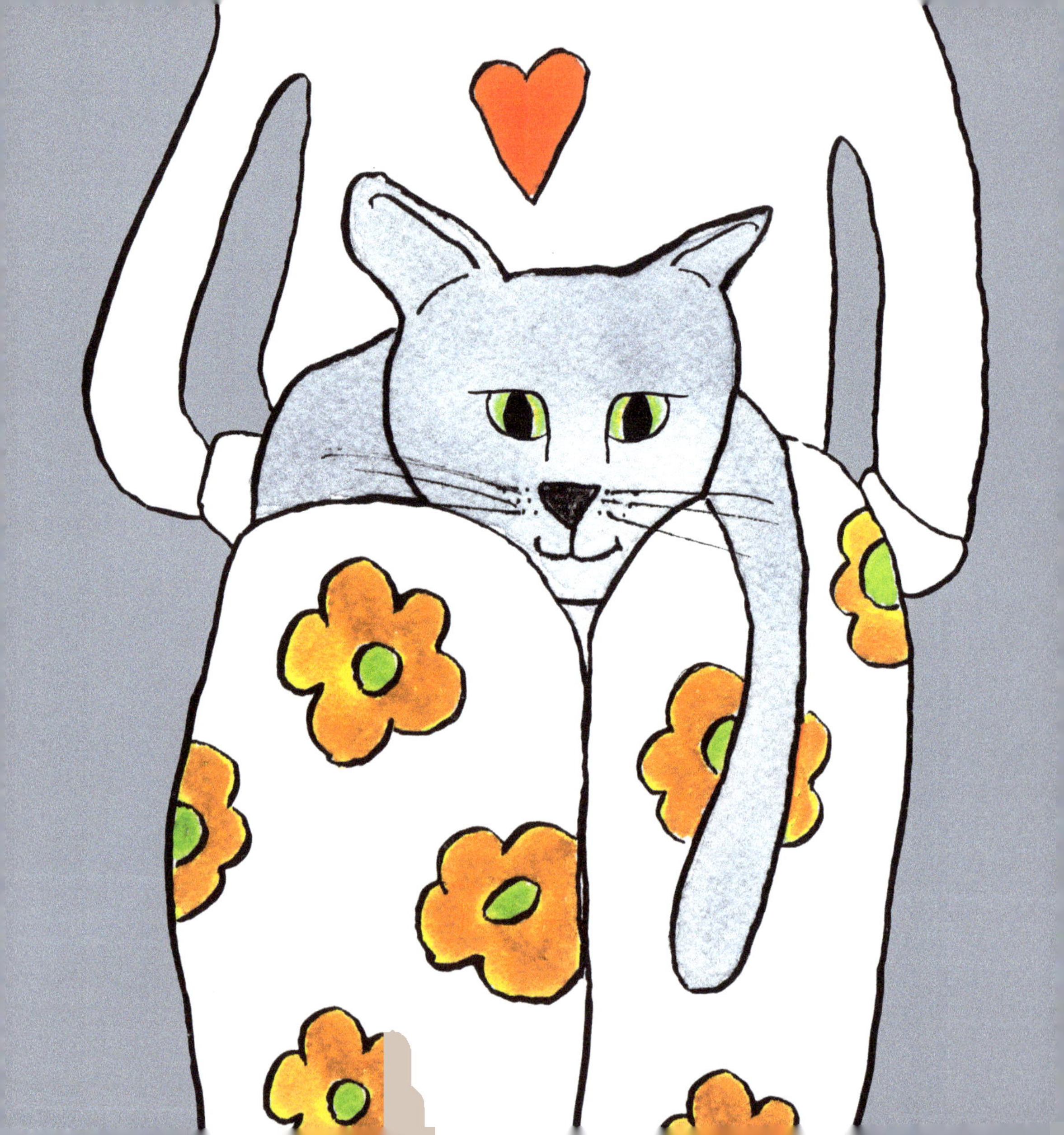

WARM HUMANS' LAPS ALL DAY LONG.

They have nothing better to do than to be your **BED** and give you a **MASSAGE**.

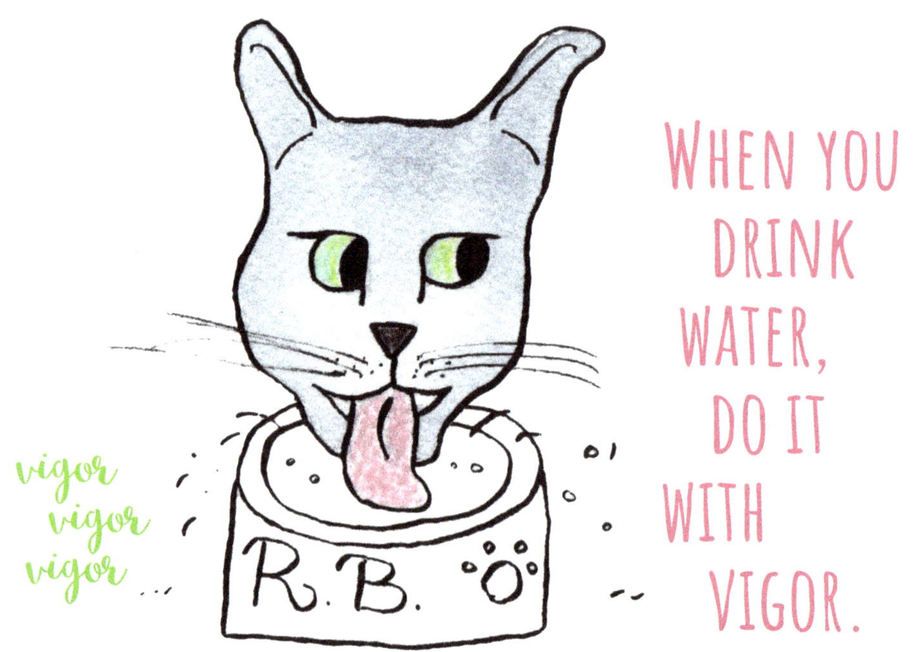

The sound of our tongues lapping up water makes them **SMILE** every time.

Some humans let you go up on the horizontal surfaces where they prepare and serve their food.

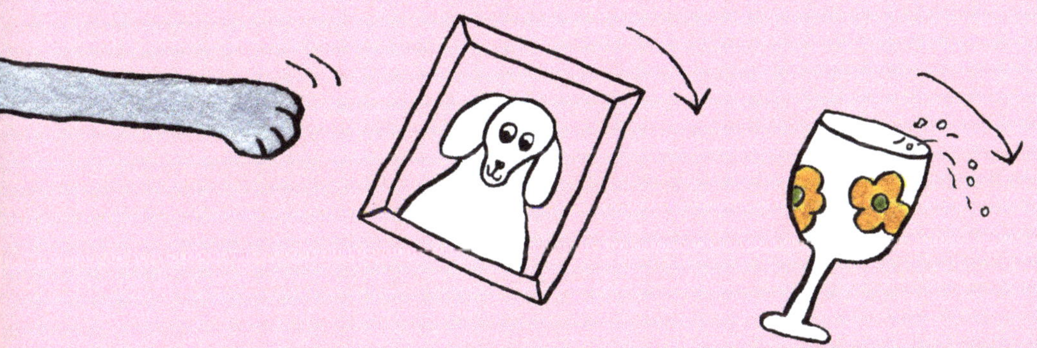

IF YOU CAN GET UP THERE, KNOCK SOMETHING DOWN. THEN, THEY'LL KNOW YOU WERE THERE.

SOME HUMANS won't let you up on the horizontal surfaces.

But, when they're not home

it's your new playground!

GO FOR IT!

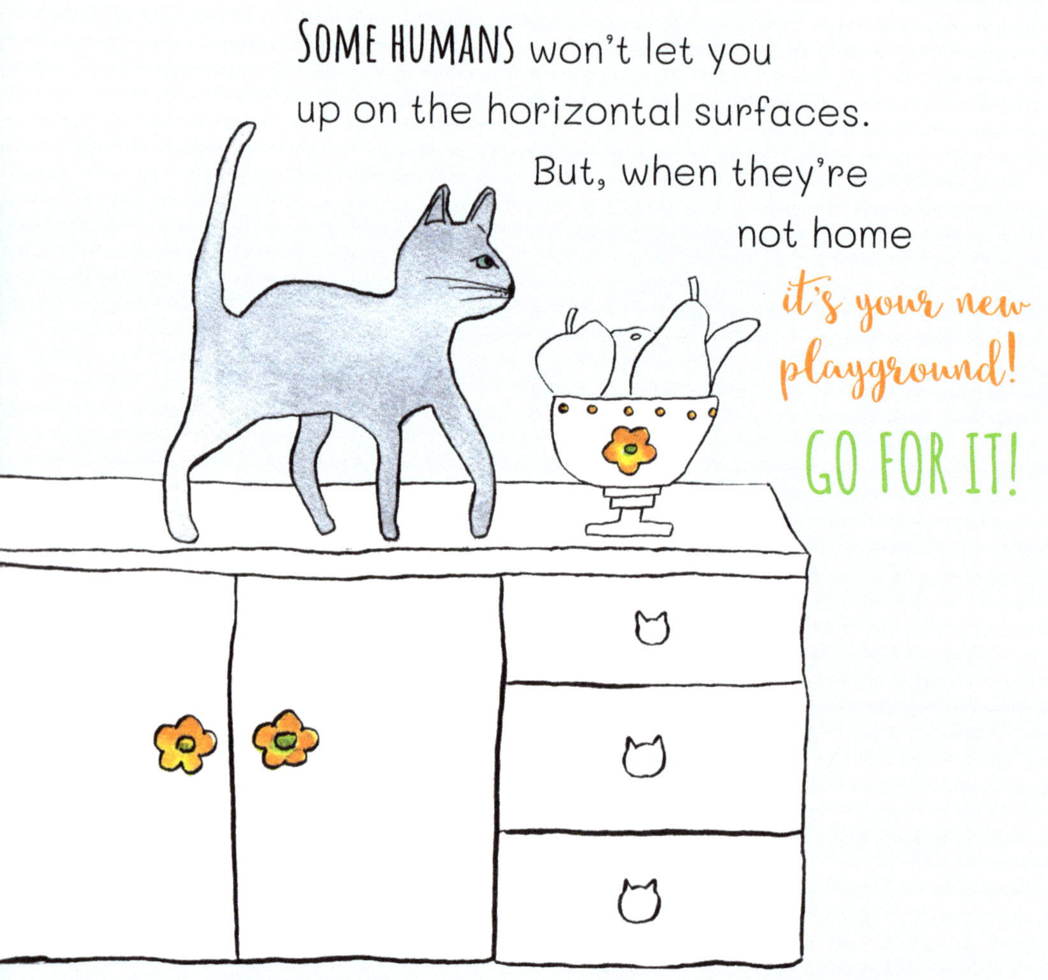

Take the *fake mice* and foam balls humans give you and lodge them under that big rectangular box where they cool food. If you're lucky, they'll use an oddly shaped metal contraption to scoop them out.

do it again. and again.

This is hours of entertainment for you!

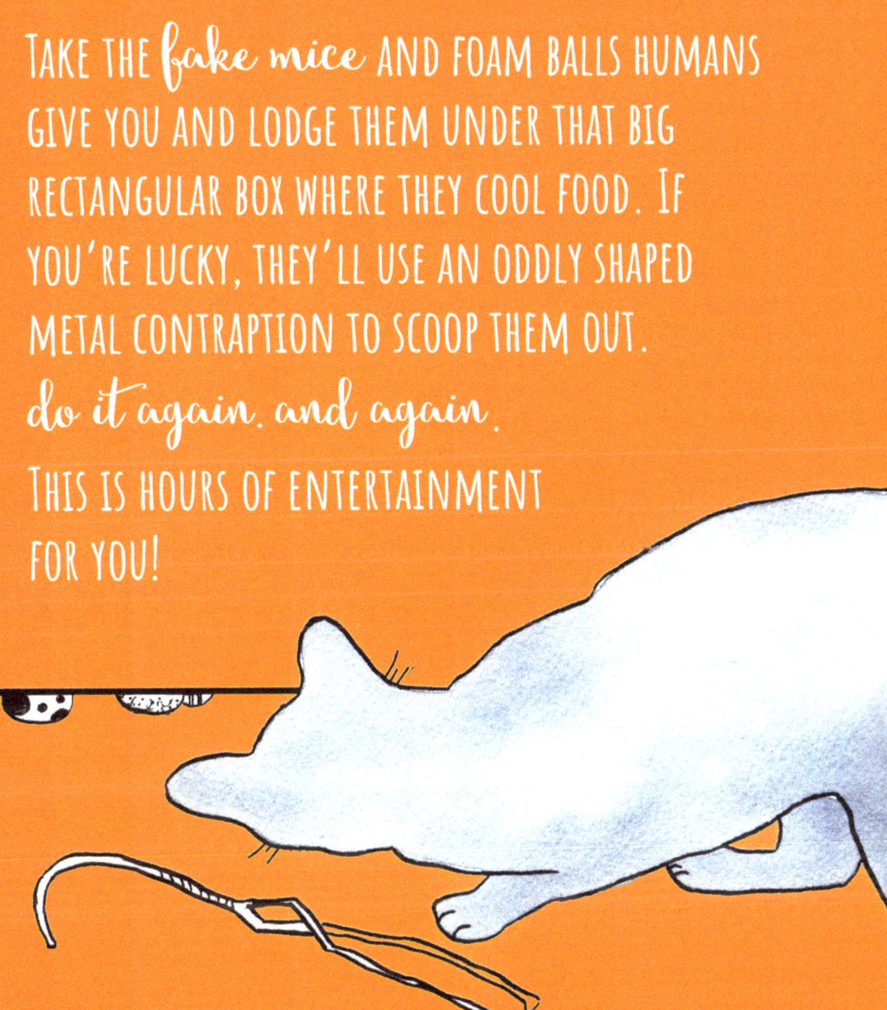

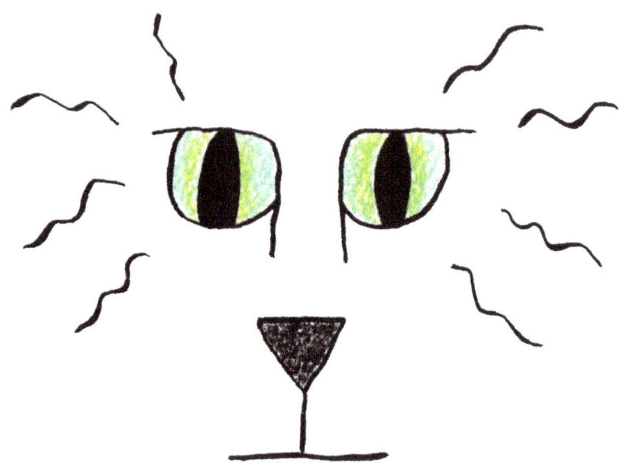

Occasionally **LOCK EYES WITH THEM** for more seconds than they are comfortable with.

YOU'LL HELP THEM PRACTICE LOOKING LOVINGLY AT OTHER COOL CATS.

Distribute lots of **LITTER** around the box where they want you to pee,

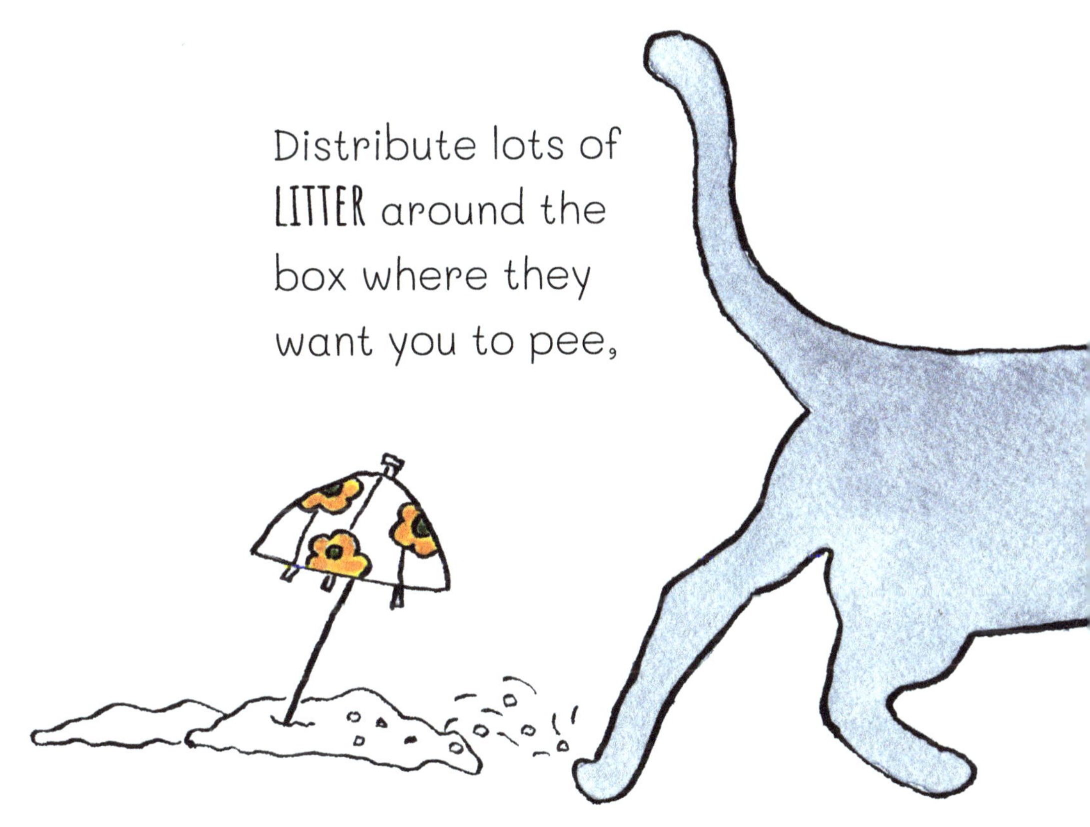

SO THEY ARE REMINDED OF *beach sand* IN BETWEEN THEIR TOES.

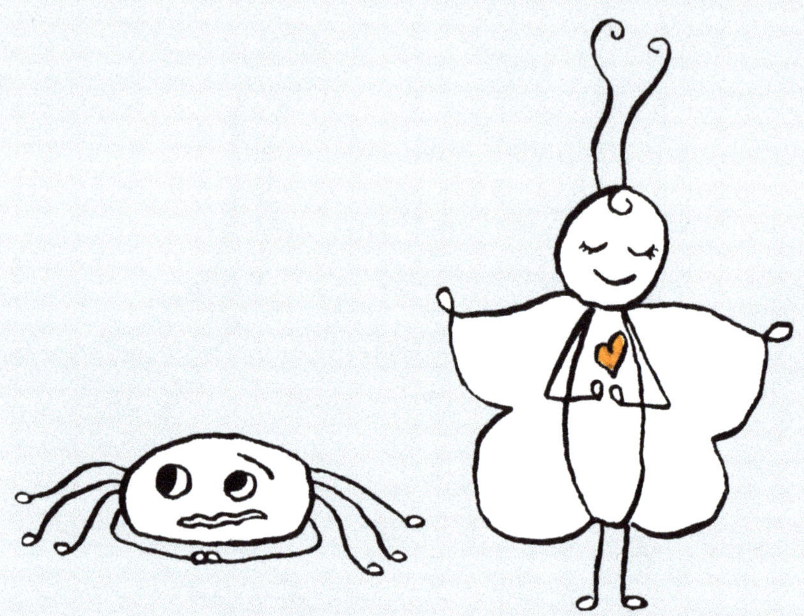

a lot of humans don't like bugs and spiders, so it's your job to **HUNT THEM DOWN.** We get to show off our animal instincts and humans don't need to call an exterminator.

IT'S A WIN-WIN.

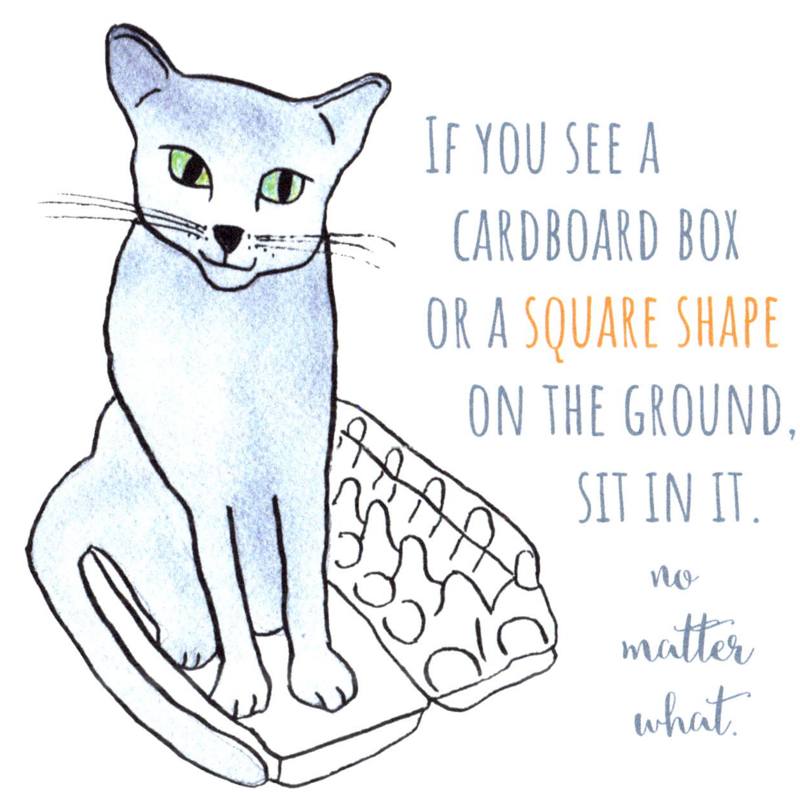

IF YOU SEE A
CARDBOARD BOX
OR A SQUARE SHAPE
ON THE GROUND,
SIT IN IT.

no
matter
what.

You're always safe in a box.

Look out the clear smooth opening in the wall to watch for flying objects with wings and creatures that are constantly scrounging for food. When you see them, eagerly wag your tail.

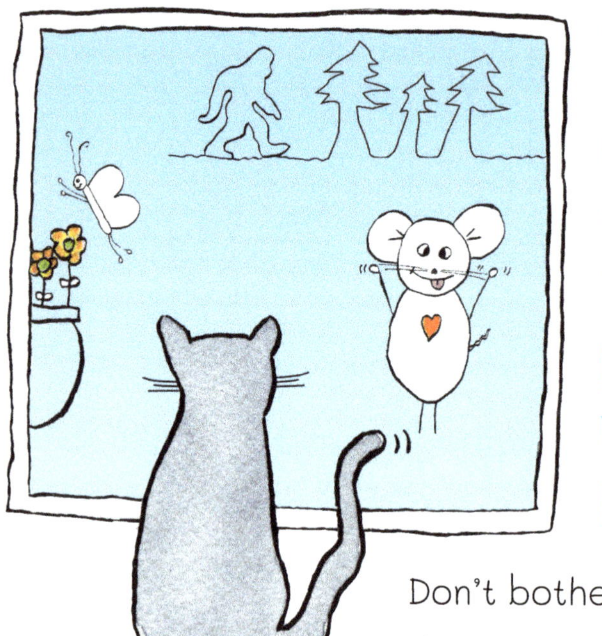

HUMANS FIND THIS CUTE AND ENTERTAINING.

Don't bother jumping into the opening though. It's just an illusion.

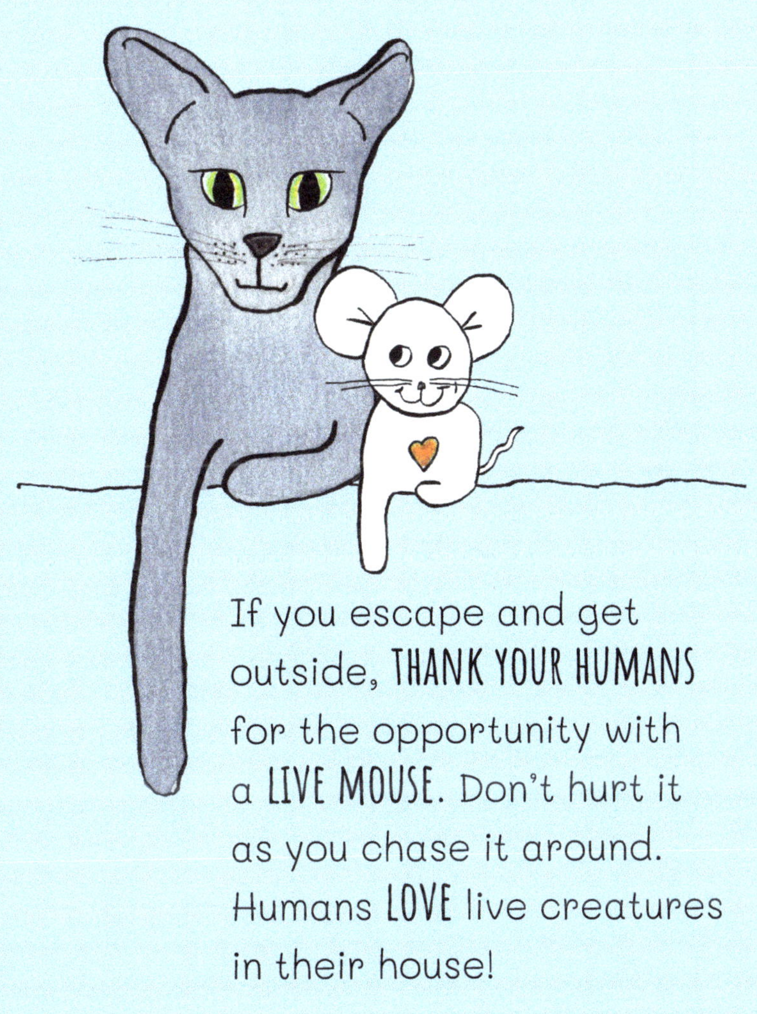

If you escape and get outside, **THANK YOUR HUMANS** for the opportunity with a **LIVE MOUSE**. Don't hurt it as you chase it around. Humans **LOVE** live creatures in their house!

Use your nails to fluff up the sides of the furniture where they like to sit. Ones with DELICATE FABRICS NEED IT THE MOST. I know this because they get so animated with their loud "*wah wah wah*" sounds when you do it.

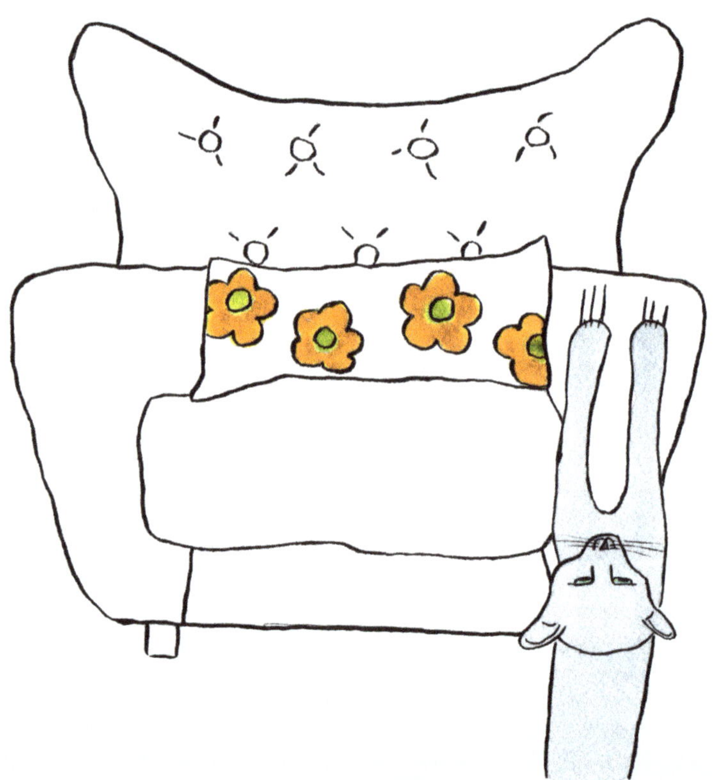

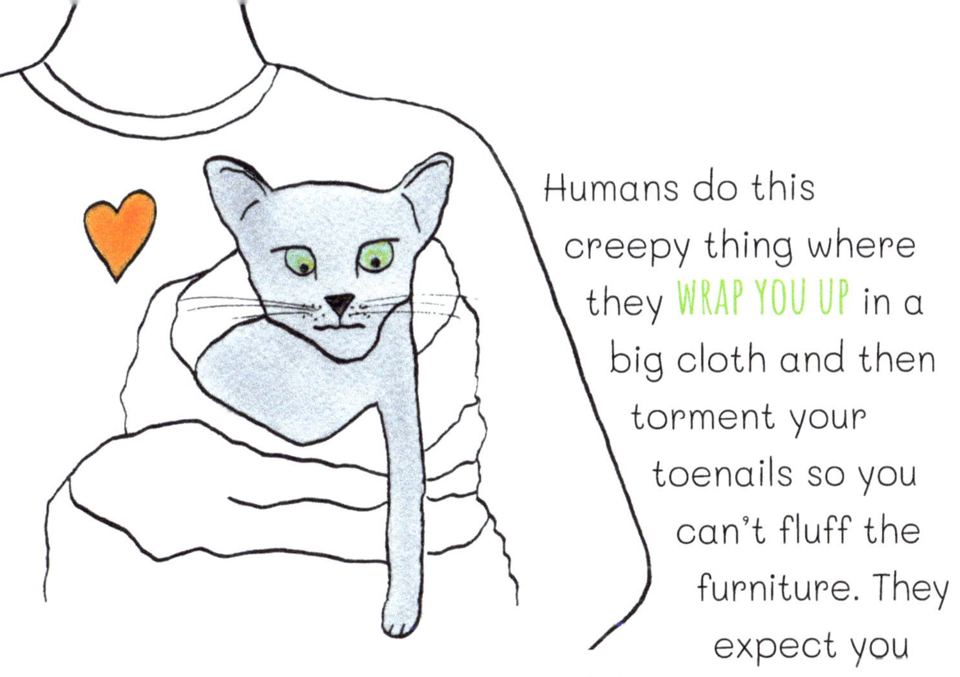

Humans do this creepy thing where they WRAP YOU UP in a big cloth and then torment your toenails so you can't fluff the furniture. They expect you to hiss and scratch. IT'S PART OF THE GAME, so don't disappoint.

WHEN THEY'RE NOT LOOKING, SCRATCH MORE FURNITURE SO YOU SHARPEN THOSE NAILS AGAIN!

Choose a few times of day where **YOU REALLY WANT ATTENTION**. They like it when you're excited, run around, **BOUNCE OFF THE FURNITURE**, and meow at them with your tail up.

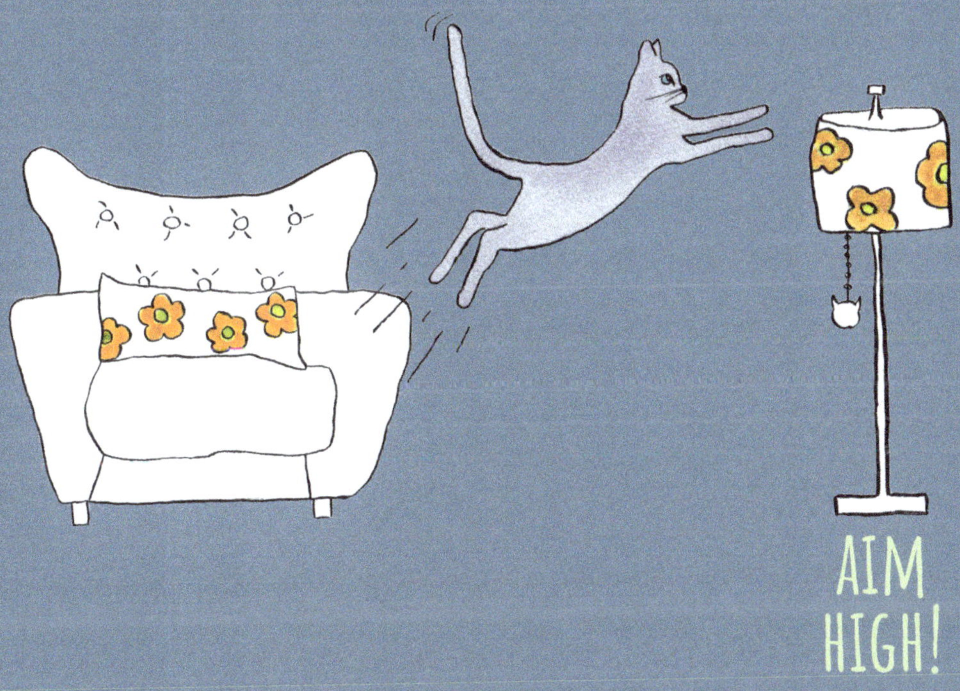
AIM
HIGH!

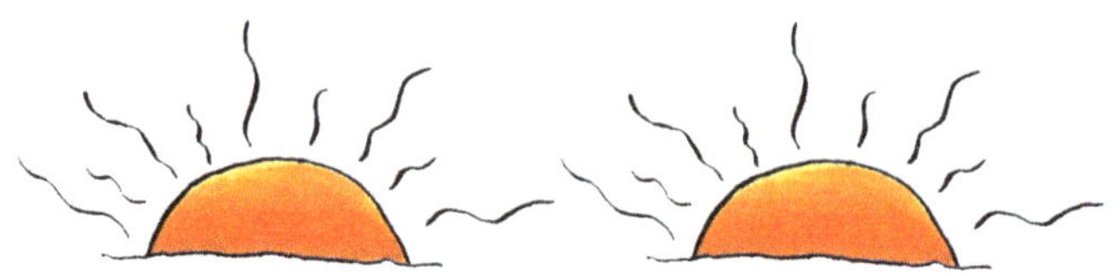

They might leave you at home
for more than TWO SUN UPS.

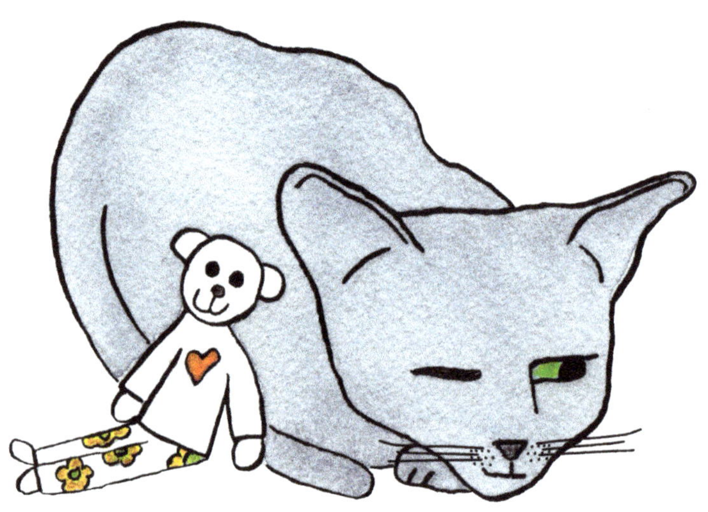

When they come back, PRETEND YOU DON'T SEE THEM for at least 2 hours.

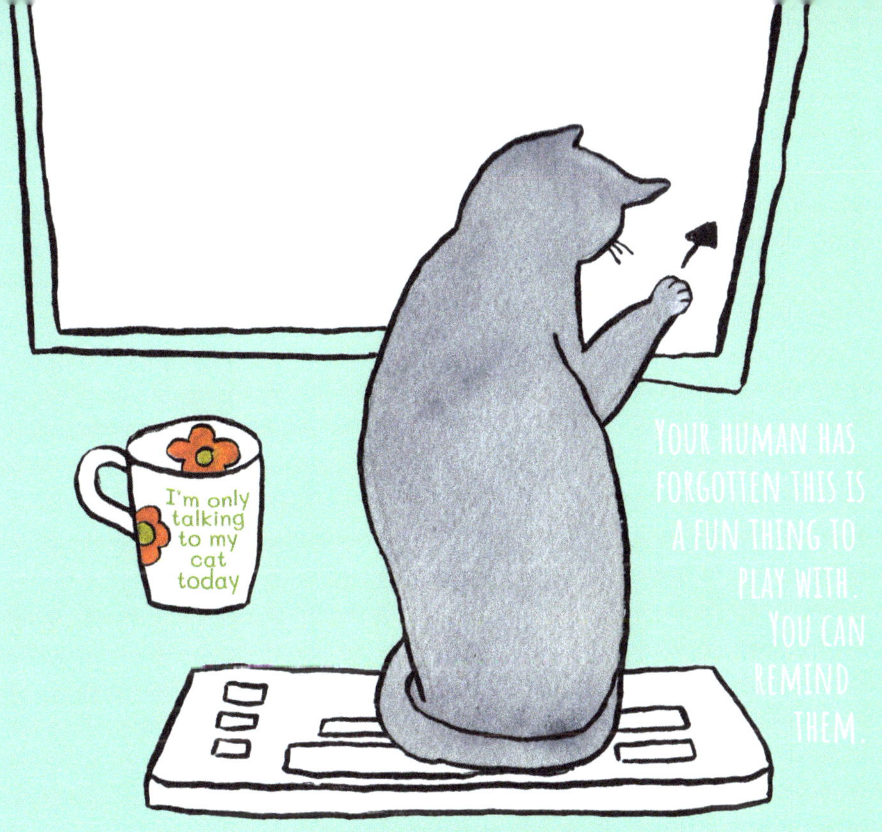

Your human has forgotten this is a fun thing to play with. You can remind them.

If you see a hard, flat rectangle of letters, SIT ON IT. Nearby there is a screen with a little black arrow on it. PAW AT THE ARROW WHILE THE HUMAN IS WORKING.

Some humans have small, robot-y **THINGS THAT MOVE** along the floor.

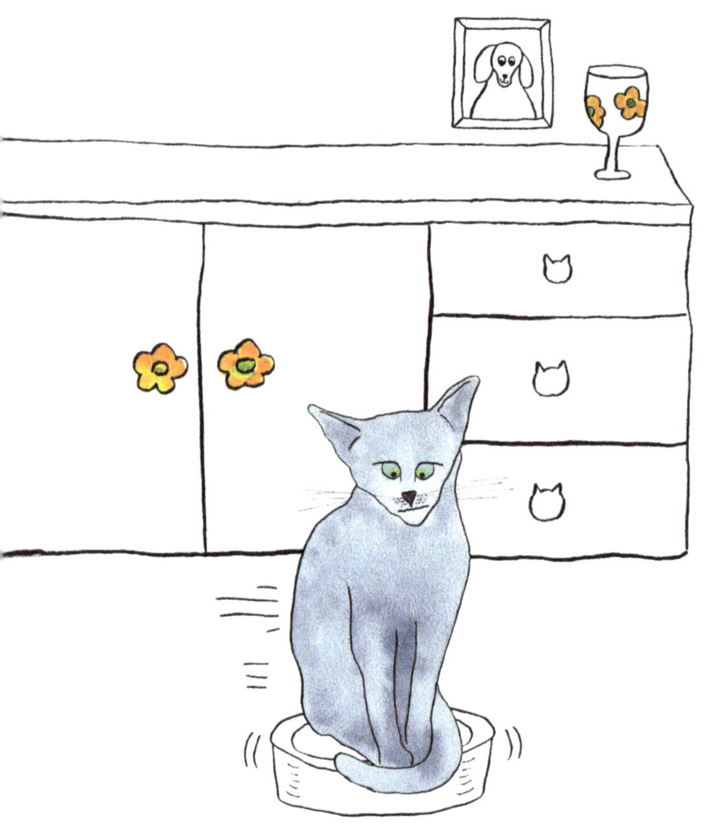

feel free to hop on every time. If you can stay there, you'll always be the hero in your human's videos.

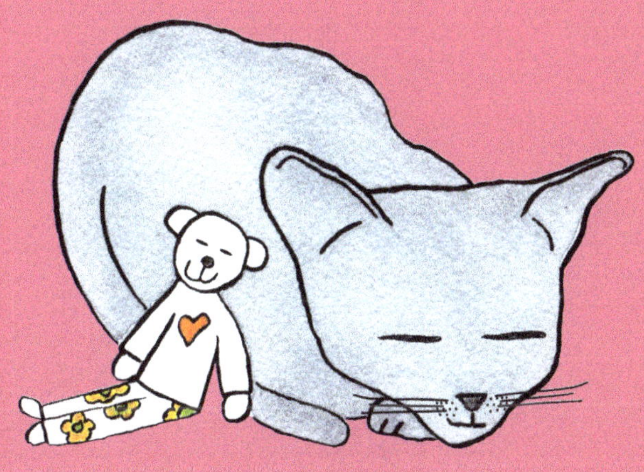

CLOSE YOUR EYES
AND NAP WHENEVER
YOU GET A CHANCE.

sleep is always an option.

If humans
call you silly
"wah wah wah"
sounds like
pumpkin, züm-diddy, or little one,
forgive them.

IT MEANS
THEY LOVE
YOU.

When you're feeling relaxed or need to *heal*, make fluttering *sounds* in your throat, half close your eyes and cross your paws. It *helps humans* relax and heal, too.

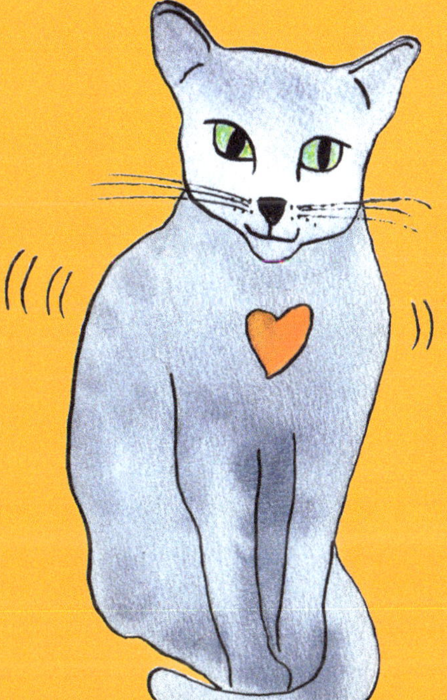

For even **FASTER HEALING**, do this while laying on their chest.

Most importantly of all...

LOVE ALL THE HUMANS.

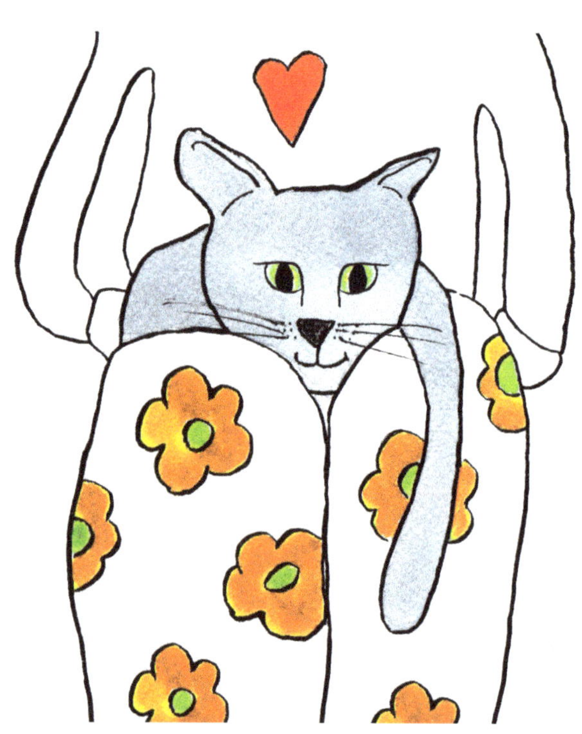

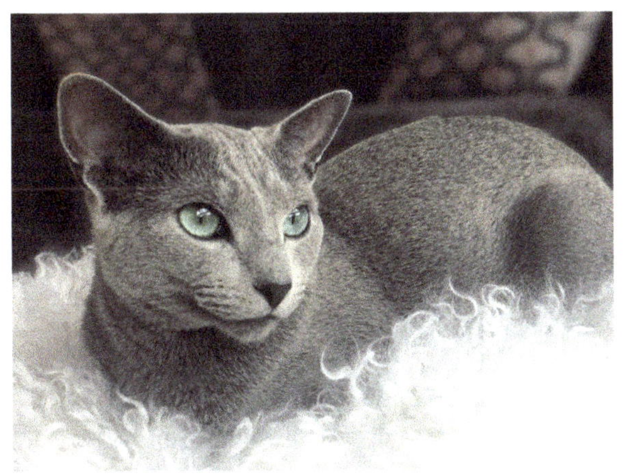

In memory of ZEN-JI, our soul mate who came in the form of a special cat. We cannot rationally explain our *connection* to him, we can only *feel* it.

"I HAVE LIVED WITH SEVERAL ZEN MASTERS – ALL OF THEM CATS."

- ECKHART TOLLE

Acknowledgements

I was not always able to take care of the cats I've had, so I'd like to recognize the **many other cool cats** who helped me take care of my Russian Blues when I traveled or moved. I hope the presence of these remarkable creatures enriched your lives, too.

To **Alex Franzen** and **Lindsey Smith**, thank you for creating a safe and supportive space for all kinds of books to launch into the world.

Thank you to **Anne Bothwell**, **Lauri Jordana** and **James McBride** who supported me through a business book idea to one that struck me out of the blue (pun intended).

Finally, a special hello to the **Daniels family** who helped me perfect a few of the tips for cool cats.

www.ingramcontent.com/pod-product-compliance
Ingram Content Group UK Ltd.
Pitfield, Milton Keynes, MK11 3LW, UK
UKHW062002290726
14090UKWH00022B/1352